NICKELODEON™

iCarly™

MAD LIBS®

by Roger Price and Leonard Stern
Based on *iCarly* created by Dan Schneider

PSS!
PRICE STERN SLOAN

PRICE STERN SLOAN
Published by the Penguin Group
Penguin Group (USA) Inc., 375 Hudson Street, New York, New York 10014, USA
Penguin Group (Canada), 90 Eglinton Avenue East, Suite 700,
Toronto, Ontario M4P 2Y3, Canada
(a division of Pearson Penguin Canada Inc.)
Penguin Books Ltd., 80 Strand, London WC2R 0RL, England
Penguin Group Ireland, 25 St. Stephen's Green, Dublin 2, Ireland
(a division of Penguin Books Ltd.)
Penguin Group (Australia), 250 Camberwell Road, Camberwell, Victoria 3124, Australia
(a division of Pearson Australia Group Pty. Ltd.)
Penguin Books India Pvt. Ltd., 11 Community Centre,
Panchsheel Park, New Delhi—110 017, India
Penguin Group (NZ), 67 Apollo Drive, Rosedale, North Shore 0632, New Zealand
(a division of Pearson New Zealand Ltd.)
Penguin Books (South Africa) (Pty.) Ltd., 24 Sturdee Avenue,
Rosebank, Johannesburg 2196, South Africa

Penguin Books Ltd., Registered Offices:
80 Strand, London WC2R 0RL, England

Published by Price Stern Sloan,
a division of Penguin Young Readers Group,
345 Hudson Street, New York, New York 10014.

ISBN 978-0-8431-3356-1

9 10

MAD LIBS®

INSTRUCTIONS

MAD LIBS® is a game for people who don't like games!
It can be played by one, two, three, four, or forty.

• RIDICULOUSLY SIMPLE DIRECTIONS

In this tablet you will find stories containing blank spaces where words are left out. One player, the READER, selects one of these stories. The READER does not tell anyone what the story is about. Instead, he/she asks the other players, the WRITERS, to give him/her words. These words are used to fill in the blank spaces in the story.

• TO PLAY

The READER asks each WRITER in turn to call out words—an adjective or a noun or whatever the space calls for—and uses them to fill in the blank spaces in the story. The result is a MAD LIBS® game.

When the READER then reads the completed MAD LIBS® game to the other players, they will discover that they have written a story that is fantastic, screamingly funny, shocking, silly, crazy, or just plain dumb—depending upon which words each WRITER called out.

• EXAMPLE (Before and After)

"_____!" he said _____
        EXCLAMATION   ADVERB

as he jumped into his convertible _____ and
                                          NOUN

drove off with his _____ wife.
                    ADJECTIVE

"_____Ouch_____!" he said _____stupidly_____
        EXCLAMATION   ADVERB

as he jumped into his convertible _____cat_____ and
                                          NOUN

drove off with his _____brave_____ wife.
                    ADJECTIVE

MAD LIBS®

QUICK REVIEW

In case you have forgotten what adjectives, adverbs, nouns, and verbs are, here is a quick review:

An ADJECTIVE describes something or somebody. *Lumpy, soft, ugly, messy,* and *short* are adjectives.

An ADVERB tells how something is done. It modifies a verb and usually ends in "ly." *Modestly, stupidly, greedily,* and *carefully* are adverbs.

A NOUN is the name of a person, place, or thing. *Sidewalk, umbrella, bridle, bathtub,* and *nose* are nouns.

A VERB is an action word. *Run, pitch, jump,* and *swim* are verbs. Put the verbs in past tense if the directions say PAST TENSE. *Ran, pitched, jumped,* and *swam* are verbs in the past tense.

When we ask for A PLACE, we mean any sort of place: a country or city *(Spain, Cleveland)* or a room *(bathroom, kitchen).*

An EXCLAMATION or SILLY WORD is any sort of funny sound, gasp, grunt, or outcry, like *Wow!, Ouch!, Whomp!, Ick!,* and *Gadzooks!*

When we ask for specific words, like a NUMBER, a COLOR, an ANIMAL, or a PART OF THE BODY, we mean a word that is one of those things, like *seven, blue, horse,* or *head.*

When we ask for a PLURAL, it means more than one. For example, *cat* pluralized is *cats.*

MAD LIBS® is fun to play with friends, but you can also play it by yourself! To begin with, DO NOT look at the story on the page below. Fill in the blanks on this page with the words called for. Then, using the words you have selected, fill in the blank spaces in the story.

Now you've created your own hilarious MAD LIBS® game!

CARLY AND SAM: BFF

ADJECTIVE _____

NUMBER _____

A PLACE _____

NOUN _____

PLURAL NOUN _____

NOUN _____

NOUN _____

PART OF THE BODY _____

PART OF THE BODY _____

NOUN _____

PART OF THE BODY _____

PLURAL NOUN _____

ADJECTIVE _____

ADJECTIVE _____

PLURAL NOUN _____

MAD LIBS

CARLY AND SAM: BFF

Carly and Sam have been _____ friends for
ADJECTIVE

_____ years. Even though Sam had a reputation throughout
NUMBER

(the) _____ for having a/an _____
A PLACE NOUN

on her shoulder, Carly, who was wise beyond her _____,
PLURAL NOUN

knew better than to judge a/an _____ by its cover.
NOUN

The girls "met" one day at lunch when Carly was eating a tuna fish

_____ and Sam yanked it right out of her
NOUN

_____. Carly took the sandwich right back, then
PART OF THE BODY

knocked Sam on her _____. "You're a/an
PART OF THE BODY

_____ after my own heart," Sam told Carly. And from
NOUN

that moment on, the two girls were joined at the _____.
PART OF THE BODY

But they definitely aren't two _____ in a pod. Carly
PLURAL NOUN

is as _____ as a cucumber while Sam has a/an
ADJECTIVE

_____ temper. But you know what they
ADJECTIVE

say—_____ attract!
PLURAL NOUN

MAD LIBS® is fun to play with friends, but you can also play it by yourself! To begin with, DO NOT look at the story on the page below. Fill in the blanks on this page with the words called for. Then, using the words you have selected, fill in the blank spaces in the story.

Now you've created your own hilarious MAD LIBS® game!

iLOVE CARLY

NOUN _____

NOUN _____

ADJECTIVE _____

ADJECTIVE _____

NOUN _____

ADVERB _____

ADJECTIVE _____

VERB _____

NUMBER _____

NOUN _____

ADVERB _____

PLURAL NOUN _____

NOUN _____

ADJECTIVE _____

PLURAL NOUN _____

PLURAL NOUN _____

VERB _____

MAD LIBS®
iLOVE CARLY

Freddie here, secretly blogging (again!) about the _____
NOUN

of my dreams, Carly Shay. She totally rocks my _____.
NOUN

I wish I could tell her right to her _____ face, but
ADJECTIVE

I get _____ butterflies in my stomach whenever I'm
ADJECTIVE

with her. What's a/an _____ to do when he's
NOUN

_____ in love with someone who just wants to
ADVERB

be _____ friends? Trouble is, Sam's always around.
ADJECTIVE

If Carly and I could _____ by ourselves it might be
VERB

different. I could tell her how I have _____ pictures of
NUMBER

her on my _____, and how _____ proud I'd be
NOUN   ADVERB

to carry her _____ home from school. I could
PLURAL NOUN

even ask her to go with me to the next school _____.
NOUN

I'd buy her a/an _____ corsage with roses and
ADJECTIVE

_____. Sigh. Why does it always seem like nice
PLURAL NOUN

_____ _____ last?
PLURAL NOUN   VERB

MAD LIBS® is fun to play with friends, but you can also play it by yourself! To begin with, DO NOT look at the story on the page below. Fill in the blanks on this page with the words called for. Then, using the words you have selected, fill in the blank spaces in the story.

Now you've created your own hilarious MAD LIBS® game!

A SPENCE-TACULAR BROTHER

A PLACE _____

VERB _____

NOUN _____

VERB ENDING IN "ING" _____

PLURAL NOUN _____

PART OF THE BODY _____

ADJECTIVE _____

ADJECTIVE _____

VERB ENDING IN "ING" _____

ANIMAL (PLURAL) _____

EXCLAMATION _____

ADJECTIVE _____

TYPE OF LIQUID _____

PLURAL NOUN _____

ADJECTIVE _____

ADJECTIVE _____

PLURAL NOUN _____

NOUN _____

NOUN _____

MAD LIBS

A SPENCE-TACULAR BROTHER

Carly thinks Spencer is the best brother in (the) _____!
A PLACE

Spencer likes to _____ to the beat of his own
VERB

_____. Whether sculpting, cooking, or _____,
NOUN   VERB ENDING IN "ING"

Spencer makes life in the loft fun. For example, he'll often

juggle _____ while standing on one _____.
PLURAL NOUN   PART OF THE BODY

He says it keeps his artistic fingers _____. When he's
ADJECTIVE

sculpting his _____ creations, he rocks out to his
ADJECTIVE

favorite band, the _____ _____. And,
VERB ENDING IN "ING"   ANIMAL (PLURAL)

_____, does he make _____ smoothies!
EXCLAMATION   ADJECTIVE

His specialty is the "Spencer Shayke," a delicious blend of frothy

_____, ripe _____, and _____ bananas.
TYPE OF LIQUID   PLURAL NOUN   ADJECTIVE

Spencer's also a/an _____ cook and enjoys serving baked
ADJECTIVE

mini meat-_____ and _____ stir fry to Carly,
PLURAL NOUN   NOUN

Sam, and Freddie in the loft—or, as he calls it, Chez Shay. Best of all,

Spencer is always willing to appear on iCarly.com, even if it means

making a complete _____ of himself—and usually, it does!
NOUN

FROM iCARLY™ MAD LIBS® • ©2008 Viacom International Inc. All Rights Reserved. Nickelodeon,
iCarly and all related titles and logos are trademarks of Viacom International Inc. Published by Price Stern Sloan,
a division of Penguin Young Readers Group, 345 Hudson Street, New York, NY 10014.

MAD LIBS® is fun to play with friends, but you can also play it by yourself! To begin with, DO NOT look at the story on the page below. Fill in the blanks on this page with the words called for. Then, using the words you have selected, fill in the blank spaces in the story.

Now you've created your own hilarious MAD LIBS® game!

¡WANT TO BE
A WEB SHOW HOST

ADJECTIVE _____

PART OF THE BODY (PLURAL) _____

PERSON IN ROOM _____

ADJECTIVE _____

COLOR _____

PLURAL NOUN _____

PART OF THE BODY _____

ADJECTIVE _____

NOUN _____

NOUN _____

PERSON IN ROOM _____

ADJECTIVE _____

ADJECTIVE _____

PLURAL NOUN _____

VERB ENDING IN "ING" _____

MAD LIBS®
iWANT TO BE
A WEB SHOW HOST

Being a good web show host is not as _____ as it

looks! Listen to what Carly and Sam have to say:

Carly: You have to be fast on your _____ and ready
PART OF THE BODY (PLURAL)

to make a joke out of anything.

Sam: Or any*one* . . . like Freddie—or _____. Thank you!
PERSON IN ROOM

Carly: You also can't be afraid to act _____. You have
ADJECTIVE

to do crazy things like paint _____ _____
COLOR   PLURAL NOUN

on your _____ with nail polish.
PART OF THE BODY

Sam: It's super important to get the timing of the _____
ADJECTIVE

effects right. For example, you need to push the laughter _____
NOUN

on the remote _____ every time you make fun of
NOUN

Freddie—or _____. And again, thank you!
PERSON IN ROOM

Carly: And you need to think up new _____ segments
ADJECTIVE

to keep the show fresh and _____. There's nothing our
ADJECTIVE

viewers like better than when we crank up the _____
PLURAL NOUN

and break into some random _____!
VERB ENDING IN "ING"

MAD LIBS® is fun to play with friends, but you can also play it by yourself! To begin with, DO NOT look at the story on the page below. Fill in the blanks on this page with the words called for. Then, using the words you have selected, fill in the blank spaces in the story.

Now you've created your own hilarious MAD LIBS® game!

THE ROLE OF A TECHNICAL PRODUCER, BY FREDDIE

SILLY WORD _____

SAME SILLY WORD _____

NOUN _____

ADJECTIVE _____

ADJECTIVE _____

ADVERB _____

ADJECTIVE _____

NOUN _____

VERB ENDING IN "ING" _____

A PLACE _____

NOUN _____

ADJECTIVE _____

ADJECTIVE _____

NOUN _____

ADJECTIVE _____

PART OF THE BODY _____

MAD LIBS®
THE ROLE OF A TECHNICAL PRODUCER, BY FREDDIE

"Testing! Testing! _____! _____!" The technical
                    SILLY WORD   SAME SILLY WORD

producer—aka me—says these words into a microphone as part

of the _____ check—one of the many _____
        NOUN   ADJECTIVE

tasks I must perform before iCarly begins. I have to make sure my

_____ camera and laptop are functioning _____.
ADJECTIVE   ADVERB

I have to program the blue screen with _____
                                        ADJECTIVE

care, enabling the background scene-changer, which can

make it look like the people on-screen are about to be eaten

by a giant _____ (which I like doing to Sam), or
            NOUN

like they're _____ across (the) _____. I
              VERB ENDING IN "ING"   A PLACE

have to be ready to fix any technical difficulties at the drop of

a/an _____ so I don't disappoint our _____
      NOUN   ADJECTIVE

viewers—and, of course, Carly. A/An _____ technical
                                      ADJECTIVE

producer always goes the extra _____ to make the
                                NOUN

hosts look _____—or, in my case, to prevent getting
            ADJECTIVE

my _____ ripped off by Sam.
    PART OF THE BODY

MAD LIBS® is fun to play with friends, but you can also play it by yourself! To begin with, DO NOT look at the story on the page below. Fill in the blanks on this page with the words called for. Then, using the words you have selected, fill in the blank spaces in the story.

Now you've created your own hilarious MAD LIBS® game!

SPENCER'S MOST MEMORABLE SCULPTURES

ADJECTIVE _____

PLURAL NOUN _____

PART OF THE BODY _____

ADJECTIVE _____

VERB ENDING IN "ING" _____

COLOR _____

PLURAL NOUN _____

NOUN _____

PLURAL NOUN _____

ADVERB _____

PART OF THE BODY _____

ADJECTIVE _____

NUMBER _____

NOUN _____

ADJECTIVE _____

PLURAL NOUN _____

MAD LIBS®
SPENCER'S MOST
MEMORABLE SCULPTURES

When it comes to creating _____ works of art
                                    ADJECTIVE

from odd _____, Spencer Shay is a master. "It's like
              PLURAL NOUN

my hands have a/an _____ of their own," he says.
                          PART OF THE BODY

His _____ sculptures include:
          ADJECTIVE

• The "Seat of _____" in the iCarly studio, which
                    VERB ENDING IN "ING"

  has flashing _____ _____ along with
                    COLOR   PLURAL NOUN

  _____-holders for snacks and beverages.
          NOUN

• The "Fan of _____," which was _____ impressive—
                  PLURAL NOUN   ADVERB

  until one flew off and nearly hit Carly in her _____.
                                                    PART OF THE BODY

• The _____ "Death to Doughnuts," which was created
            ADJECTIVE

  from _____ doughnuts and decorated using a
              NUMBER

  paintball _____.
                  NOUN

While he's truly a/an _____ artist, Spencer does have
                            ADJECTIVE

one problem: Everything he creates, even if it's non-electrical, seems

to burst into _____!
                  PLURAL NOUN

MAD LIBS® is fun to play with friends, but you can also play it by yourself! To begin with, DO NOT look at the story on the page below. Fill in the blanks on this page with the words called for. Then, using the words you have selected, fill in the blank spaces in the story.

Now you've created your own hilarious MAD LIBS® game!

SPECIAL SEGMENTS ON iCARLY.COM, PART 1

ADJECTIVE _____

VERB ENDING IN "ING" _____

PLURAL NOUN _____

PLURAL NOUN _____

PLURAL NOUN _____

PLURAL NOUN _____

VERB _____

ADJECTIVE _____

PERSON IN ROOM _____

SAME PERSON IN ROOM _____

ADJECTIVE _____

TYPE OF LIQUID _____

NOUN _____

ADJECTIVE _____

PLURAL NOUN _____

ADJECTIVE _____

PLURAL NOUN _____

TYPE OF FOOD _____

TYPE OF FOOD _____

MAD LIBS®
SPECIAL SEGMENTS ON iCARLY.COM, PART 1

_____ segments like these keep iCarly.com viewers
<small>ADJECTIVE</small>

_____ back for more!
<small>VERB ENDING IN "ING"</small>

- "Random Debates": Which is better: _____ or
<small>PLURAL NOUN</small>

_____? Sam and Freddie argue the pros
<small>PLURAL NOUN</small>

and _____ of both, and viewers vote.
<small>PLURAL NOUN</small>

- "iWanna Rock": Sam and Carly grab their favorite air _____,
<small>PLURAL NOUN</small>

_____ up the volume, and get down with their
<small>VERB</small>

_____ selves.
<small>ADJECTIVE</small>

- "Eat, _____, Eat!": Watch as _____
<small>PERSON IN ROOM</small>   <small>SAME PERSON IN ROOM</small>

samples _____ culinary mixtures such as
<small>ADJECTIVE</small>

_____ over _____ chunks.
<small>TYPE OF LIQUID</small>   <small>NOUN</small>

- "iCrush It": Stand back! Spencer runs in with a/an _____
<small>ADJECTIVE</small>

sledgehammer and crushes things into teeny-tiny _____.
<small>PLURAL NOUN</small>

- "Hey, What Am I Sitting On?": Spencer plants his _____
<small>ADJECTIVE</small>

butt in the Chair of _____ to guess if he's
<small>PLURAL NOUN</small>

sitting on _____ or _____.
<small>TYPE OF FOOD</small>   <small>TYPE OF FOOD</small>

MAD LIBS® is fun to play with friends, but you can also play it by yourself! To begin with, DO NOT look at the story on the page below. Fill in the blanks on this page with the words called for. Then, using the words you have selected, fill in the blank spaces in the story.

Now you've created your own hilarious MAD LIBS® game!

SPECIAL SEGMENTS ON iCARLY.COM, PART 2

ADJECTIVE _____

VERB ENDING IN "ING" _____

ADJECTIVE _____

NOUN _____

NOUN _____

PLURAL NOUN _____

ADJECTIVE _____

PART OF THE BODY _____

NOUN _____

NOUN _____

VERB ENDING IN "ING" _____

PLURAL NOUN _____

SAME PLURAL NOUN _____

PLURAL NOUN _____

ADJECTIVE _____

MAD LIBS®
SPECIAL SEGMENTS ON iCARLY.COM, PART 2

More of the _____ segments that make iCarly.com
                    ADJECTIVE

viewers burst out _____:
                  VERB ENDING IN "ING"

• "iFlush It": Carly and Sam see what exactly can be flushed down

  a/an _____ toilet. A/An _____?
        ADJECTIVE   NOUN

  Or perhaps a/an _____?
                    NOUN

• "Sam Orders Food": After phoning in an order for some hot

  _____, Sam puts a/an _____
       PLURAL NOUN   ADJECTIVE

  mask over her _____ and scares the
                  PART OF THE BODY

  _____ out of the delivery _____ so
    NOUN   NOUN

  he runs from the room _____.
                         VERB ENDING IN "ING"

• "_____ in My Pants": How many _____
    PLURAL NOUN   SAME PLURAL NOUN

  can be stuffed into Freddie's _____? (Caution:
                                 PLURAL NOUN

  Carly and Sam are _____ professionals. Do not
                      ADJECTIVE

  try this at home.)

MAD LIBS® is fun to play with friends, but you can also play it by yourself! To begin with, DO NOT look at the story on the page below. Fill in the blanks on this page with the words called for. Then, using the words you have selected, fill in the blank spaces in the story.

Now you've created your own hilarious MAD LIBS® game!

TEXT US AT iCARLY.COM

PART OF THE BODY (PLURAL) _____

ADJECTIVE _____

PLURAL NOUN _____

PLURAL NOUN _____

PLURAL NOUN _____

ADJECTIVE _____

PLURAL NOUN _____

ADJECTIVE _____

PART OF THE BODY _____

PLURAL NOUN _____

TYPE OF FOOD _____

CELEBRITY_____

PART OF THE BODY _____

ADJECTIVE _____

PERSON IN ROOM _____

ADJECTIVE _____

PART OF THE BODY _____

NOUN _____

MAD LIBS®

TEXT US AT iCARLY.COM

Inquiring _____ want to know what
                         PART OF THE BODY (PLURAL)

_____ iCarly.com fans are saying! Check out some of
     ADJECTIVE

our recently posted text _____:
                       PLURAL NOUN

- 4EverFriends: What's up, my _____? My _____
                                  PLURAL NOUN   PLURAL NOUN

  and I love to watch your _____ show while sitting in
                             ADJECTIVE

  our beanbag _____.
               PLURAL NOUN

- FlirtyGirl: I wish Freddie could be my _____ boyfriend.
                                  ADJECTIVE

  He's a total _____-throb. Hugs and _____!
           PART OF THE BODY   PLURAL NOUN

- _____-Lover: Hey, can you invite _____
     TYPE OF FOOD   CELEBRITY

  on the show to _____ wrestle with Spencer?
                   PART OF THE BODY

  That would be so _____ to watch!
                   ADJECTIVE

- FlipFlopChick: Hey, iCarly and iSam—_____
                                 PERSON IN ROOM

  here! U R 2 _____! I laugh my _____ off at
             ADJECTIVE   PART OF THE BODY

  you guys. Keep up the great _____!
                        NOUN

MAD LIBS® is fun to play with friends, but you can also play it by yourself! To begin with, DO NOT look at the story on the page below. Fill in the blanks on this page with the words called for. Then, using the words you have selected, fill in the blank spaces in the story.

Now you've created your own hilarious MAD LIBS® game!

PROMOTING YOUR WEB SHOW

PLURAL NOUN _____

ADJECTIVE _____

PART OF THE BODY (PLURAL) _____

ADJECTIVE _____

PERSON IN ROOM _____

NOUN _____

A PLACE _____

ADJECTIVE _____

ARTICLE OF CLOTHING (PLURAL) _____

CELEBRITY_____

NUMBER _____

ADJECTIVE _____

ADJECTIVE _____

NOUN _____

PLURAL NOUN _____

MAD LIBS®

PROMOTING YOUR WEB SHOW

So how do you get more _____ watching your
PLURAL NOUN

_____ web show? Carly, Sam, and Freddie put their
ADJECTIVE

_____ together and came up with lots of
PART OF THE BODY (PLURAL)

_____ ideas:
ADJECTIVE

1. Carly and Sam could ask the coolest kid in school—

_____—to appear on iCarly.com as a guest _____
PERSON IN ROOM   NOUN

and give away a trip to (the) _____.
A PLACE

2. Carly and Sam could wear _____
ADJECTIVE

_____ with a picture of _____
ARTICLE OF CLOTHING (PLURAL)   CELEBRITY

saying "I ❤ iCarly.com" to school every day for _____
NUMBER

weeks.

3. Freddie could tape Spencer leading the Ridgeway cheerleaders

in a/an _____ cheer about iCarly.com at the
ADJECTIVE

next pep rally. (After all, who wouldn't want to see Spencer looking

_____ wearing a pleated _____
ADJECTIVE   NOUN

and cheering with pom-_____!)
PLURAL NOUN

MAD LIBS® is fun to play with friends, but you can also play it by yourself! To begin with, DO NOT look at the story on the page below. Fill in the blanks on this page with the words called for. Then, using the words you have selected, fill in the blank spaces in the story.

Now you've created your own hilarious MAD LIBS® game!

IN THE HALLWAYS OF RIDGEWAY

ADJECTIVE _____

A PLACE _____

ADJECTIVE _____

PLURAL NOUN _____

ADJECTIVE _____

TYPE OF FOOD (PLURAL) _____

TYPE OF LIQUID _____

ANIMAL _____

SILLY WORD _____

PERSON IN ROOM (MALE) _____

PERSON IN ROOM _____

VERB ENDING IN "ING" _____

PERSON IN ROOM _____

ADJECTIVE _____

PLURAL NOUN _____

ADJECTIVE _____

VERB _____

PLURAL NOUN _____

ADJECTIVE _____

PLURAL NOUN _____

TYPE OF LIQUID _____

MAD LIBS®
IN THE HALLWAYS
OF RIDGEWAY

Hey there, Carly here, live from my _____ school.
                                      ADJECTIVE

Located near (the) _____, Ridgeway is like any other
                        A PLACE

_____ school. It has its jocks, brains, geeks, and
     ADJECTIVE

_____—and _____ cafeteria food like
   PLURAL NOUN   ADJECTIVE

mashed _____ swimming in _____. Our
         TYPE OF FOOD (PLURAL)   TYPE OF LIQUID

mascot is a/an _____ named Sir _____. The cutest
                    ANIMAL   SILLY WORD

boy in school is _____. "Germy" _____ is
                 PERSON IN ROOM (MALE)   PERSON IN ROOM

always coughing and _____ on the other kids. "Rip-off"
                      VERB ENDING IN "ING"

_____ sells _____ _____. Our
 PERSON IN ROOM   ADJECTIVE   PLURAL NOUN

principal is super _____, but some of the teachers
                        ADJECTIVE

make you want to _____ away and never come back.
                        VERB

Miss Briggs enjoys making our _____ miserable, and Mr.
                                  PLURAL NOUN

Howard hands out _____ detentions whenever we
                      ADJECTIVE

slam our _____ too loudly. Oh well, I'll survive. After all,
          PLURAL NOUN

when life gives you lemons, you just make some _____!
                                                  TYPE OF LIQUID

MAD LIBS® is fun to play with friends, but you can also play it by yourself! To begin with, DO NOT look at the story on the page below. Fill in the blanks on this page with the words called for. Then, using the words you have selected, fill in the blank spaces in the story.

Now you've created your own hilarious MAD LIBS® game!

¡WANT TO BE A GUEST HOST

PLURAL NOUN _____

NOUN _____

NOUN _____

NUMBER _____

PERSON IN ROOM (MALE) _____

A PLACE _____

NOUN _____

PERSON IN ROOM _____

A PLACE _____

NUMBER _____

NOUN _____

NUMBER _____

PERSON IN ROOM _____

A PLACE _____

NOUN _____

TYPE OF LIQUID _____

VERB ENDING IN "ING" _____

ADJECTIVE _____

ADJECTIVE _____

MAD LIBS®

¡WANT TO BE A GUEST HOST

As all of you iCarly.com _____ out there know, we're
                        PLURAL NOUN

giving one lucky _____ the chance to be our cohost
                        NOUN

for one episode. To be considered, viewers had to submit videos

of themselves doing something totally out of this _____.
                                                        NOUN

We received over _____ entries, and our finalists are:
                    NUMBER

- _____ from (the) _____, who put on a
  PERSON IN ROOM (MALE)   A PLACE

  pink frilly _____ and asked his crush on a date.
                  NOUN

- _____ from (the) _____, who ate
  PERSON IN ROOM   A PLACE

  _____ peanut butter and _____ sandwiches
      NUMBER   NOUN

  in _____ seconds.
        NUMBER

- _____ from (the) _____, who put on a bathing
  PERSON IN ROOM   A PLACE

  _____ and went scuba diving in a vat of _____.
      NOUN   TYPE OF LIQUID

And for our viewers' _____ pleasure, these
                        VERB ENDING IN "ING"

_____ finalists will audition live on our next episode of
    ADJECTIVE

iCarly.com. So be there—or be _____!
                                    ADJECTIVE

MAD LIBS® is fun to play with friends, but you can also play it by yourself! To begin with, DO NOT look at the story on the page below. Fill in the blanks on this page with the words called for. Then, using the words you have selected, fill in the blank spaces in the story.

Now you've created your own hilarious MAD LIBS® game!

ODE TO FOOD, BY SAM

NOUN _____

TYPE OF FOOD _____

TYPE OF LIQUID _____

VERB ENDING IN "ING" _____

ADJECTIVE _____

TYPE OF FOOD (PLURAL) _____

NOUN _____

ADVERB _____

PART OF THE BODY _____

SILLY WORD _____

NOUN _____

NOUN _____

ADJECTIVE _____

ADJECTIVE _____

NOUN _____

VERB _____

NOUN _____

PLURAL NOUN _____

PLURAL NOUN _____

PLURAL NOUN _____

NOUN _____

MAD LIBS®

ODE TO FOOD, BY SAM

I am Sam. I love ham—and bacon, _____ jerky, fried

NOUN

_____, and popcorn topped with warm _____.

TYPE OF FOOD ⟶ TYPE OF LIQUID

I like eating as much as I like _____ with Carly.

VERB ENDING IN "ING"

(But not Freddie—he's a/an _____ doof.) Anyway, all

ADJECTIVE

work and no _____ makes me one cranky

TYPE OF FOOD (PLURAL)

_____. In fact, whenever I'm _____

NOUN ⟶ ADVERB

hungry, my _____ doesn't just grumble—it shouts

PART OF THE BODY

"_____!" I love eating at Carly's _____

SILLY WORD ⟶ NOUN

because Spencer is an awesome _____. His _____

NOUN ⟶ ADJECTIVE

tacos and his _____ homemade pasta á la _____

ADJECTIVE ⟶ NOUN

are simply to-_____-for! If it's true that the way to a

VERB

girl's _____ is through her stomach, then bring me a

NOUN

bowl of cheesy _____, a box of barbecue _____,

PLURAL NOUN ⟶ PLURAL NOUN

or a bunch of chocolate-covered _____. Mmmmmmm.

PLURAL NOUN

Just the thought gives me the _____-bumps!

NOUN

MAD LIBS® is fun to play with friends, but you can also play it by yourself! To begin with, DO NOT look at the story on the page below. Fill in the blanks on this page with the words called for. Then, using the words you have selected, fill in the blank spaces in the story.

Now you've created your own hilarious MAD LIBS® game!

DEAR DAD:
AN E-MAIL FROM CARLY

A PLACE _____

ADVERB _____

ADJECTIVE _____

NOUN _____

ADJECTIVE _____

PLURAL NOUN _____

ADJECTIVE _____

PLURAL NOUN _____

NOUN _____

PLURAL NOUN _____

VERB _____

ADJECTIVE _____

NUMBER _____

ADJECTIVE _____

NOUN _____

TYPE OF FOOD _____

VERB _____

PLURAL NOUN _____

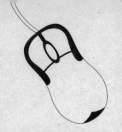

MAD LIBS®
DEAR DAD:
AN E-MAIL FROM CARLY

Hi, Dad. How are things in (the) _____? Spencer
                                      A PLACE

and I miss you _____! Don't worry. He's taking
                     ADVERB

_____ care of me. He makes sure I get on the school
   ADJECTIVE

_____ every morning and finish my _____
   NOUN   ADJECTIVE

homework every night. In fact, you'll be pleased to know I'm getting

straight _____ in all my _____ classes!
         PLURAL NOUN   ADJECTIVE

Spencer also insists I eat three square _____ a day,
                                            PLURAL NOUN

make my _____ when I get up, and put all my dirty
            NOUN

_____ in the dishwasher. But he lets me have fun, too.
   PLURAL NOUN

Sam and I have _____ -overs all the time. We go to
                     VERB

_____ Smoothies at least _____ times a
   ADJECTIVE   NUMBER

week. And, of course, we still do iCarly with Freddie. Spencer's also

been working on some _____ masterpieces lately. His latest
                          ADJECTIVE

creation is a giant _____ made from _____!
                        NOUN   TYPE OF FOOD

Got to go—time to film iCarly. _____ soon, okay?
                                     VERB

All my _____, Carly
           PLURAL NOUN

MAD LIBS® is fun to play with friends, but you can also play it by yourself! To begin with, DO NOT look at the story on the page below. Fill in the blanks on this page with the words called for. Then, using the words you have selected, fill in the blank spaces in the story.

Now you've created your own hilarious MAD LIBS® game!

BEST VIEWER-SUBMITTED VIDEOS, PART 1

ADVERB _____

ADJECTIVE _____

NUMBER _____

ADJECTIVE _____

NOUN _____

CELEBRITY_____

ADVERB _____

PLURAL NOUN _____

PLURAL NOUN _____

PLURAL NOUN _____

ADJECTIVE _____

PERSON IN ROOM _____

TYPE OF LIQUID _____

PLURAL NOUN _____

MAD LIBS®
BEST VIEWER-SUBMITTED VIDEOS, PART 1

Carly, Sam, and Freddie are often _____ shocked at the
                                        ADVERB

_____ things viewers will film themselves doing to get on
ADJECTIVE

iCarly.com. In the past, viewers have recorded themselves:

• chewing _____ pieces of bubblegum and blowing a/an
                NUMBER

_____ bubble in the shape of a/an _____.
ADJECTIVE   NOUN

• forging _____'s name and handing out _____
              CELEBRITY   ADVERB

autographed _____.
                  PLURAL NOUN

• making a pizza topped with _____ and extra
                                    PLURAL NOUN

_____ and delivering it to your _____
PLURAL NOUN   ADJECTIVE

next-door neighbor, _____.
                        PERSON IN ROOM

• filling balloons with _____ and throwing them at
                            TYPE OF LIQUID

unsuspecting _____.
                PLURAL NOUN

MAD LIBS® is fun to play with friends, but you can also play it by yourself! To begin with, DO NOT look at the story on the page below. Fill in the blanks on this page with the words called for. Then, using the words you have selected, fill in the blank spaces in the story.

Now you've created your own hilarious MAD LIBS® game!

BEST VIEWER-SUBMITTED VIDEOS, PART 2

ADJECTIVE _____

COLOR _____

ARTICLE OF CLOTHING _____

PLURAL NOUN _____

PLURAL NOUN _____

VERB _____

CELEBRITY_____

NOUN _____

NOUN _____

NOUN _____

PLURAL NOUN _____

NOUN _____

VERB ENDING IN "ING"_____

ADVERB _____

PLURAL NOUN _____

MAD LIBS®
BEST VIEWER-SUBMITTED VIDEOS, PART 2

More _____ antics from iCarly.com fans! Their videos
       ADJECTIVE

show them:

- picking out a fuzzy _____ _____ at the
                 COLOR   ARTICLE OF CLOTHING

  store and asking the clerk if she will accept either _____
                                          PLURAL NOUN

  or _____ as payment.
     PLURAL NOUN

- going through a _____-thru and asking if _____
                VERB   CELEBRITY

  is working there today.

- stopping an unsuspecting _____ on the street and
                          NOUN

  telling him they're reporters for the local TV _____
                                     NOUN

  and are conducting a "_____ on the Street" interview.
                 NOUN

- announcing to a crowd of _____ that they just won
                          PLURAL NOUN

  the gold _____ in the World _____
            NOUN   VERB ENDING IN "ING"

  Championships, then bowing and _____ tossing
                              ADVERB

  _____ into the crowd.
    PLURAL NOUN

MAD LIBS® is fun to play with friends, but you can also play it by yourself! To begin with, DO NOT look at the story on the page below. Fill in the blanks on this page with the words called for. Then, using the words you have selected, fill in the blank spaces in the story.

Now you've created your own hilarious MAD LIBS® game!

FIGHTING WORDS

PLURAL NOUN _____

PLURAL NOUN _____

ADJECTIVE _____

NOUN _____

NOUN _____

ADJECTIVE _____

ADJECTIVE _____

ADJECTIVE _____

ADVERB _____

TYPE OF FOOD _____

PART OF THE BODY _____

NOUN _____

NOUN _____

NOUN _____

PLURAL NOUN _____

NOUN _____

NOUN _____

ADJECTIVE _____

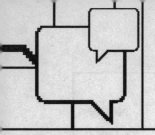

MAD LIBS
FIGHTING WORDS

Lace up your boxing _____ and listen as Sam and
                        PLURAL NOUN

Freddie fight like cats and _____:
                            PLURAL NOUN

Sam: Freddie, it's a/an _____ shame you're such a
                           ADJECTIVE

techno-_____. Since you can't get Carly—or any other
        NOUN

cute _____—to go out with you, you can always hang out
     NOUN

with your _____ laptop in your _____ room.
          ADJECTIVE   ADJECTIVE

Freddie: If you think being the butt of your _____ jokes
                                                 ADJECTIVE

gets to me, Sam, you're _____ mistaken.
                        ADVERB

Sam: You smell like rotten _____!
                               TYPE OF FOOD

Freddie: Look who's talking. Your _____ is shaped like
                                      PART OF THE BODY

a/an _____.
     NOUN

Sam: Stick a/an _____ in it, you _____, or
                    NOUN   NOUN

I'll beat the _____ outta you!
              PLURAL NOUN

Freddie: You know, Sam, a girl usually teases a _____
                                                    NOUN

when she likes him. But even if you were the last _____
                                                  NOUN

on earth, I'd still prefer my _____ laptop.
                              ADJECTIVE

MAD LIBS® is fun to play with friends, but you can also play it by yourself! To begin with, DO NOT look at the story on the page below. Fill in the blanks on this page with the words called for. Then, using the words you have selected, fill in the blank spaces in the story.

Now you've created your own hilarious MAD LIBS® game!

A VISIT TO THE JUNKYARD

NOUN _____

NOUN _____

ADJECTIVE _____

VERB _____

ADJECTIVE _____

PLURAL NOUN _____

ADJECTIVE _____

SILLY WORD _____

PLURAL NOUN _____

ANIMAL _____

NOUN _____

PART OF THE BODY (PLURAL) _____

NOUN _____

PART OF THE BODY _____

ADJECTIVE _____

NOUN _____

PART OF THE BODY (PLURAL) _____

NOUN _____

MAD LIBS®

A VISIT TO THE JUNKYARD

Greetings, fellow _____-lings. It is I, Spencer Shay, doing
             NOUN

a remote for iCarly.com at the local junk-_____. This is
                                    NOUN

my _____ place—it's where I go whenever I need artistic
    ADJECTIVE

inspiration to _____. Investigating the _____
            VERB   ADJECTIVE

piles of _____ here at the junkyard always gives me
        PLURAL NOUN

_____ sculpture ideas. _____, look here! It's a
  ADJECTIVE   SILLY WORD

dozen silver-plated _____. Yes! I can melt them down and
               PLURAL NOUN

pour the silver over this discarded old stuffed teddy _____
                                             ANIMAL

I just found. I'll call it "Silver and Old." Genius! Holy _____,
                                          NOUN

check this out. I can't believe my _____!
                                  PART OF THE BODY (PLURAL)

It's a vintage disco _____! I'll put photos of
                            NOUN

my _____ all over it and call it "Spencer the
        PART OF THE BODY

_____: Supreme _____ of Planet
      ADJECTIVE   NOUN

Jam." There's so much here at the junkyard that it makes me weak in

the _____. It's true what they say: One man's
      PART OF THE BODY (PLURAL)

trash is another man's _____!
                  NOUN

FROM iCARLY™ MAD LIBS® • ©2008 Viacom International Inc. All Rights Reserved. Nickelodeon,
iCarly and all related titles and logos are trademarks of Viacom International Inc. Published by Price Stern Sloan,
a division of Penguin Young Readers Group, 345 Hudson Street, New York, NY 10014.

MAD LIBS® is fun to play with friends, but you can also play it by yourself! To begin with, DO NOT look at the story on the page below. Fill in the blanks on this page with the words called for. Then, using the words you have selected, fill in the blank spaces in the story.

Now you've created your own hilarious MAD LIBS® game!

NEVELOCITY.COM

PLURAL NOUN _____

ADJECTIVE _____

PART OF THE BODY _____

ADJECTIVE _____

ADJECTIVE _____

PLURAL NOUN _____

ADJECTIVE _____

TYPE OF LIQUID _____

ANIMAL _____

ADJECTIVE _____

NOUN _____

NOUN _____

VERB _____

TYPE OF FOOD _____

PART OF THE BODY _____

ADJECTIVE _____

PART OF THE BODY (PLURAL) _____

The unthinkable has happened, my dear _____.
PLURAL NOUN

I've found something I despise even more than germs—a/an

_____ web show called iCarly. Even the most potent
ADJECTIVE

_____-sanitizer couldn't clean up the _____ act
PART OF THE BODY   ADJECTIVE

of the show's _____ cohost, Carly Shay. In fact, if you're
ADJECTIVE

trying to decide between watching iCarly.com and doing anything

else—playing video _____, reading a/an _____
PLURAL NOUN   ADJECTIVE

book, having a cup of _____ with friends—let me
TYPE OF LIQUID

suggest any one of those. Frankly, feeding time at the _____
ANIMAL

cage at the zoo is more entertaining. But let me be perfectly

_____: I am *not* just trashing iCarly.com because Carly
ADJECTIVE

refused to pucker up and give me a/an _____. Or
NOUN

because when I smelled her _____ and asked her to
NOUN

_____ with me, she smeared _____ dip all
VERB   TYPE OF FOOD

over my _____. No, it's because iCarly.com is unworthy.
PART OF THE BODY

In fact, I give it two _____ _____ down!
ADJECTIVE   PART OF THE BODY (PLURAL)

FROM iCARLY™ MAD LIBS® • ©2008 Viacom International Inc. All Rights Reserved. Nickelodeon,
iCarly and all related titles and logos are trademarks of Viacom International Inc. Published by Price Stern Sloan,
a division of Penguin Young Readers Group, 345 Hudson Street, New York, NY 10014.

MAD LIBS® is fun to play with friends, but you can also play it by yourself! To begin with, DO NOT look at the story on the page below. Fill in the blanks on this page with the words called for. Then, using the words you have selected, fill in the blank spaces in the story.

Now you've created your own hilarious MAD LIBS® game!

¡GET IN TROUBLE . . . A LOT!

NOUN _____

NOUN _____

NUMBER _____

NOUN _____

PERSON IN ROOM (MALE) _____

PART OF THE BODY _____

PLURAL NOUN _____

ADJECTIVE _____

NOUN _____

ADJECTIVE _____

PLURAL NOUN _____

ADJECTIVE _____

TYPE OF LIQUID _____

VERB (PAST TENSE) _____

PART OF THE BODY _____

MAD LIBS®
¡GET IN TROUBLE . . . A LOT!

Sam has been sent to the principal's _____ so many
$\quad\quad\quad\quad\quad\quad\quad\quad\quad\quad\quad\quad\quad\quad$ NOUN

times, she's on a first-_____ basis with him. In fact, she's
$\quad\quad\quad\quad\quad\quad\quad\quad$ NOUN

already gotten _____ detentions this year for:
$\quad\quad\quad\quad\quad\quad$ NUMBER

• throwing a/an _____ in the hallway and accidentally
$\quad\quad\quad\quad\quad\quad\quad\quad$ NOUN

hitting _____ in the _____,
$\quad\quad$ PERSON IN ROOM (MALE) $\quad\quad\quad\quad$ PART OF THE BODY

knocking him down a flight of _____.
$\quad\quad\quad\quad\quad\quad\quad\quad\quad$ PLURAL NOUN

• putting up posters with Miss Briggs's _____ head on
$\quad\quad\quad\quad\quad\quad\quad\quad\quad\quad\quad\quad$ ADJECTIVE

the body of a wild _____.
$\quad\quad\quad\quad\quad$ NOUN

• taping _____ _____ all over Principal
$\quad\quad\quad$ ADJECTIVE $\quad\quad\quad\quad$ PLURAL NOUN

Franklin's car.

• sneaking into Miss Briggs's house and replacing her _____
$\quad\quad\quad\quad\quad\quad\quad\quad\quad\quad\quad\quad\quad\quad\quad$ ADJECTIVE

shampoo with _____.
$\quad\quad\quad\quad$ TYPE OF LIQUID

• asking Mr. Howard who _____ and left him in
$\quad\quad\quad\quad\quad\quad\quad$ VERB (PAST TENSE)

charge—and then spray painting his _____.
$\quad\quad\quad\quad\quad\quad\quad\quad\quad\quad$ PART OF THE BODY

MAD LIBS® is fun to play with friends, but you can also play it by yourself! To begin with, DO NOT look at the story on the page below. Fill in the blanks on this page with the words called for. Then, using the words you have selected, fill in the blank spaces in the story.

Now you've created your own hilarious MAD LIBS® game!

LOOPY LEWBERT

ADJECTIVE _____

EXCLAMATION _____

NOUN _____

PART OF THE BODY _____

NOUN _____

TYPE OF LIQUID _____

ADJECTIVE _____

NOUN _____

VERB (PAST TENSE) _____

PLURAL NOUN _____

NOUN _____

VERB ENDING IN "ING" _____

NOUN _____

ADJECTIVE _____

CELEBRITY (FEMALE) _____

SAME CELEBRITY (FEMALE) _____

NOUN _____

NOUN _____

MAD LIBS
LOOPY LEWBERT

Lewbert is the _____ doorman in Carly and Freddie's
ADJECTIVE

building—and, _____, he is one crabby _____!
EXCLAMATION NOUN

Possibly because he has a mole on his _____ that's the
PART OF THE BODY

size of a small _____. Spencer and Carly are sure it's filled
NOUN

with gooey _____. He has a really _____
TYPE OF LIQUID ADJECTIVE

temper. He blows his _____ if anyone messes up his
NOUN

lobby floor after he's just _____. And whenever there
VERB (PAST TENSE)

are a lot of _____ in the lobby, he'll throw a temper
PLURAL NOUN

_____. This led Carly and Sam to create a segment on
NOUN

iCarly.com called "_____ with Lewbert" where
VERB ENDING IN "ING"

they do obnoxious things to drive Lewbert up the _____.
NOUN

For example, they'll call him in the lobby and blast a/an

_____ airhorn into the phone. Or they'll hide his prized
ADJECTIVE

photo of _____, causing him to run around yelling,
CELEBRITY (FEMALE)

"_____, my precious _____, wherefore
SAME CELEBRITY (FEMALE) NOUN

art thou?" Yep, ol' Lewbert is definitely off his _____!
NOUN